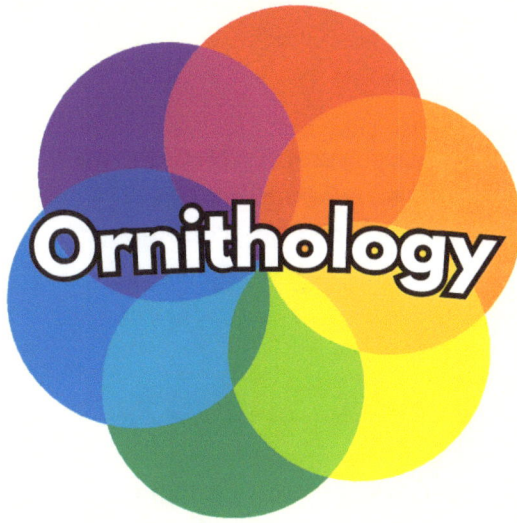

Ornithology

Book of COLORS

Nature's Bird Rainbow

AO PRESS

Jessica Lee Anderson

Paperback ISBN: 978-1-964078-25-0

To Seth, Grant, Scot, and Anita, thanks for sharing your love of birds with us! - JLA

Photo credits, left to right, top to bottom: Front cover (Keel-billed toucan): swisshippo; Interior cover (Peach-faced lovebirds): Life on White; Copyright page (chicks): LivingImages; Dedication page: Farinosa; p. 4: Neil Bowman, brentawp, Skyler Erwing; p. 5: BirdImages, brentawp, Phiphat Suwanmon, ihorga; p. 6: BirdImages, SweetyMommy, Anolis01; p. 7: matthewo2000, kimmik69, cascoly; p. 8: Steve Byland, hailshadow, tupungato; p. 9: Slavisa Tomanovic, Pria_Berkasima, Jeffry S.S.; p. 10: Brian Lasenby, puksamran, Alotom; p. 11: drferry, webguzs, krishnendu; p. 12: BecCreeper, christels, Martine Blanchette; p. 13: Stefonlinton, Kyle Robinson, Bilanol; p. 14: alphotographic, Pedro Ferreira, Birdimages; p. 15: nialot, Alfonso Chen, drferry; p. 16: Wirestock, drferry, Tina Nord; p. 17: Banu R, Rudolph Ernst;, lightpix; p. 18: Ralph Blechschmidt, BrianEKushner, migleon; p. 19: Lily Estachio, eyewave, Brittany Crossman; p. 20: OldFulica, zanskar, Jillian Cooper; p. 21: Peter Charlesworth, Anneliese Gruenwald-Maerkl, complex; p. 22: Frank Hildebrand, Mr. Jamesy, rpbirdman; p. 23: User4c1fb51d_286, Murengstockphoto, Harris Collins; p. 24: panumat, Mason Maron, Westhoff; p. 25: Timothy Loyd, Neil Bowman, Life on White; p. 26: PavelS, bdfyjdbx, Petr Polak; p. 27: Ken Canning, Daniel Jara, AndChisPhoto; p. 28: mantaphoto, Karel Bock, feathercollector; p. 29: jedgcomb, William Warby, Harry Collins; p. 30: IanZa, nreflect, ygluzberg; p. 31: kajornyot, rageracer1988, Freder; p. 32: Arie Hoogzand, David McGowen, Ondrej Prosicky; p. 33: Ken Griffiths, ozflash; Michel Viard; p. 34: Michael Anderson; Back cover (European bird-eaters): drakuliren

This Book Belongs to:

_____

Ornithology is the study of birds.

Cockatiel

Red

Flame-colored tanager

Vermillion flycatcher

Birds come in all shapes, colors, and sizes.

Northern cardinal

Red

Summer tanager

Birds have feathers and wings, and most species can fly!

Ruddy kingfisher

Scarlet ibis

Orange

Rufous hummingbird

Bullock's oriole

Instead of teeth, birds have beaks that can be different shapes and sizes.

Sun parakeets

Orange

Carolina wren

Orange canary

Andean cock-of-the-rock

Some birds eat seeds, fruits, and nuts while other types of birds eat insects, fish, and animals.

Yellow

Yellow warbler

Saffron finch

Birds all have feathers! Feathers help birds to stay warm and dry, plus they can be used to fly and also show off!

Golden conure

Yellow

Eurasian golden oriole

Parakeets (budgies)

Golden pheasant

Bird feathers are made out of keratin, just like your nails and hair.

Green

Glistening-green tanager

Green broadbill

All types of birds lay eggs! Eggs are covered in a shell that protects the babies as they develop.

Emerald toucanet

Green

Green-crowned brilliant

Turaco

Rose-ringed parakeet

Bird eggs come in a variety of sizes, and they can take weeks or even months to hatch.

Blue

There are thousands of known bird species with new species still being discovered!

Splendid fairy wren

Blue macaw

Blue jay

Blue

Mountain bluebird

Birds can be found all over the world in both wild and urban areas.

Indigo bunting

Little blue heron

Purple

All birds have bony skeletons, and many have hollow bones, an important feature for birds that can fly.

Violet-backed starling

Purple grenadier

Purple martin

Purple

Common grackle

Shapes and structures vary between species (and even within the same species)!

Violet sabrewing hummingbird

Varied bunting

Pink

Anna's hummingbird

Pink robin

Birds can have different wing shapes, and some are built for speed, soaring, or hovering.

Roseate spoonbill

Pink

Pink cockatoos

Some birds will migrate, or travel great distances during seasons, to find food, build nests, or to locate other resources.

Rosy pelican (great white pelican)

Flamingos

Black

Black silkie chicken

American coot

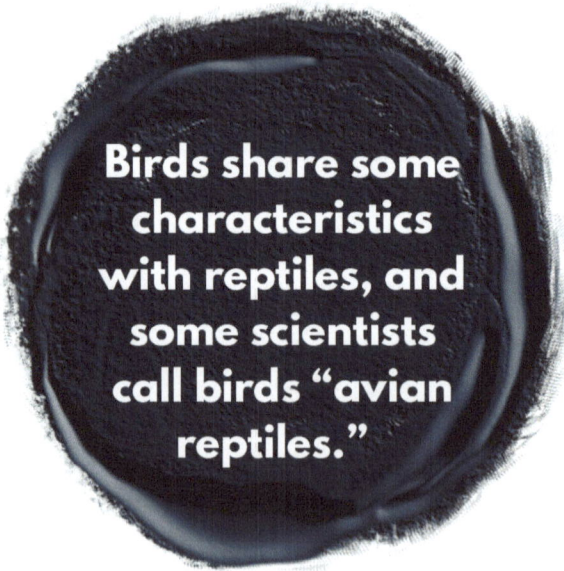

Birds share some characteristics with reptiles, and some scientists call birds "avian reptiles."

Black vultures

Black

Double-crested cormorant

Unlike reptiles, birds are "warm-blooded" (their body temperature stays constant, even in cold weather).

Common raven

American crow

White

Snowy egret

Ivory gull

Scientific studies show that birds are intelligent and can use tools as well as solve problems.

Snowy owl

White

Cockatoo

Sebastopol goose

White swan

Birds have complex social behaviors and can communicate through a wide variety of sounds.

Gray

Gray catbird

Tufted titmouse

Certain colors can help birds blend into their environment (camouflage).

Mourning doves

Gray

Greylag goose

African gray parrot

Great gray owl

Birds molt (or shed old feathers and grow new ones) at least once a year.

Brown

Brown falcon

Black-footed albatross

Birds live in a variety of habitats like forests, wetlands, grasslands, and deserts.

Wild turkey

Brown

Great horned owl

Smoky-brown woodpecker

North Island brown kiwi

Birds are important—they control pests, spread seeds, pollinate, and bring delight to many people!

COLOR Combinations

Can you describe the colors and patterns of these large bird species?

Ostrich

Cassowary

Emu

COLOR Combinations

Bald eagle

How are these birds of prey similar and different when it comes to colors, shapes, and patterns?

Golden eagle

Secretary birds

COLOR Combinations

Can you describe the colors and patterns of these birds?

Vulturine guinea fowl

Wood duck

Swinhoe's pheasant

COLOR Combinations

Lilac-breasted roller

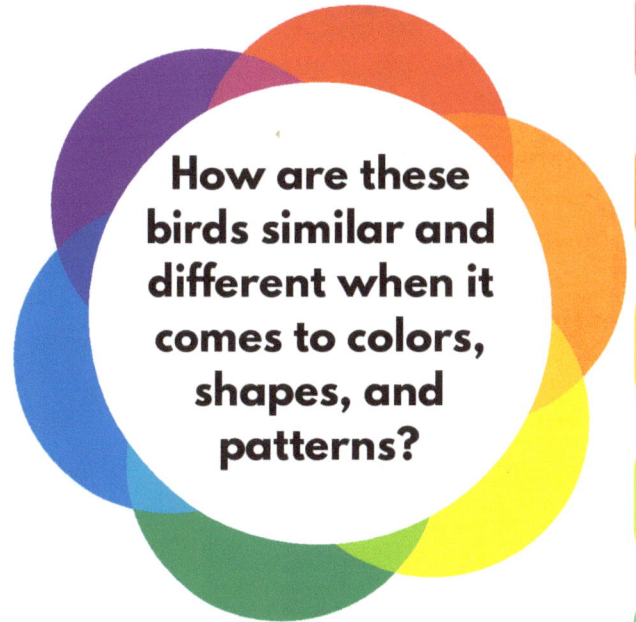

How are these birds similar and different when it comes to colors, shapes, and patterns?

Gouldian finch

Fiery-throated hummingbird

COLOR Combinations

Cape starling bird

Peacock

What are some colors and features you notice about these birds? What do you think they do?

American purple gallinule

COLOR Combinations

Black-backed kingfisher

How are these birds similar and different when it comes to colors, shapes, and patterns?

Rainbow lorikeets

Scarlet macaw

COLOR Combinations

Crimson rosella

Painted bunting

What are some similarities and differences you observe in the colors and features of these birds?

Resplendent quetzal

COLOR Combinations

Rock hopper penguins

What are the colors, shapes, and physical properties of these penguins? How are they the same or different?

Fairy penguin

Emperor penguins

Jessica Lee Anderson is an award-winning author of over 75 books for young readers including the NAOMI NASH chapter book series. Jessica loves spending time in nature and exploring the outdoors with her husband, Michael, and their daughter, Ava! Jessica loves finding colorful birds near her home in Austin, Texas. You can learn more about Jessica by visiting www.jessicaleeanderson.com.

Check out these other books:

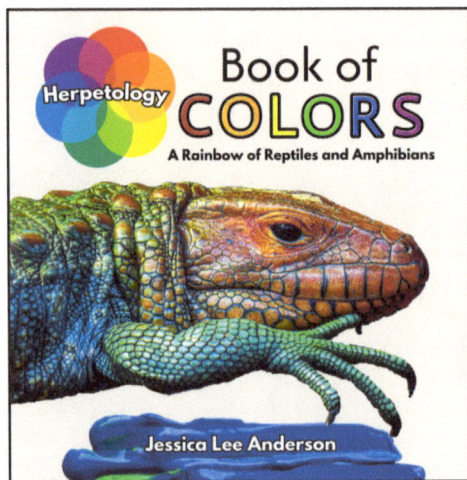

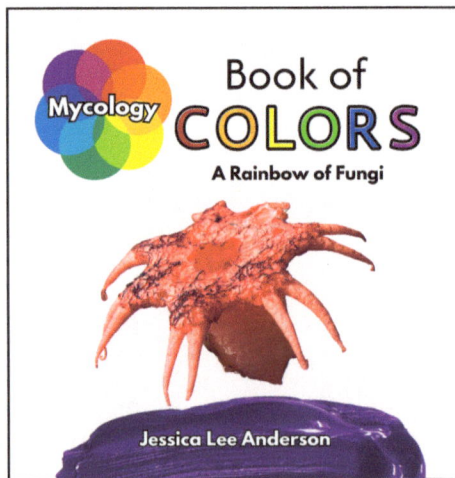

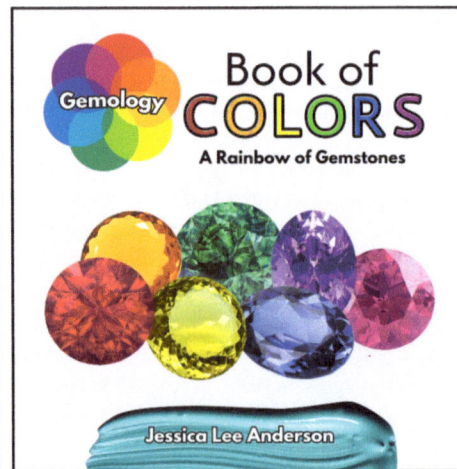

Herpetology **Book of COLORS**
A Rainbow of Reptiles and Amphibians
Jessica Lee Anderson

Mycology **Book of COLORS**
A Rainbow of Fungi
Jessica Lee Anderson

Gemology **Book of COLORS**
A Rainbow of Gemstones
Jessica Lee Anderson

www.ingramcontent.com/pod-product-compliance
Lightning Source LLC
Chambersburg PA
CBHW061145030426
42335CB00002B/107